Also by James White

Hi, Let's Go Fishing, Volume I

Hi, Let's Go Fishing, Volume II

Withstanding Storms That Surround

Peace Easy

A Personal Story of Faith and Dealing with
Attention Deficit Disorder

JAMES CLARENCE WHITE

WestBow
PRESS
A DIVISION OF THOMAS NELSON

WestBow Press books may be ordered through booksellers or by contacting:

WestBow Press
A Division of Thomas Nelson
1663 Liberty Drive
Bloomington, IN 47403
www.westbowpress.com
1-(866) 928-1240

Because of the dynamic nature of the Internet, any web addresses or links contained in this book may have changed since publication and may no longer be valid. The views expressed in this work are solely those of the author and do not necessarily reflect the views of the publisher, and the publisher hereby disclaims any responsibility for them.

Any people depicted in stock imagery provided by Thinkstock are models, and such images are being used for illustrative purposes only.

Certain stock imagery © Thinkstock.

ISBN: 978-1-4497-4472-4 (hc)
ISBN: 978-1-4497-4471-7 (sc)
ISBN: 978-1-4497-4470-0 (e)

Library of Congress Control Number: 2012905685

Printed in the United States of America

WestBow Press rev. date: 03/30/2012

Contents

Preface xi

Acknowledgments xiii

Introduction xv

1 Grammar School 1

2 High School 9

3 College Undergraduate (Phase I) 25

4 College Undergraduate: The Turnaround (Phase II) ... 35

5 College Undergraduate: Donna (Phase III) 39

6 The Land of the Great Graduate School (Phase IV) ... 57

7 The Return Home (Phase V) 71

Epilogue 75

About the Author 85

For Holden

I am going to send an angel in front of you, to guard you on the way and to bring you to the place that I have prepare

—Exodus 23:20 (NRSV)

'For surely I know the plans I have for you,' says the Lord, 'plans for your welfare and not for harm, to give you a future with hope.'

—Jeremiah 29:11 (NRSV)

Preface

Many stories have been, and remain to be, written about individuals who have overcome difficult circumstances. The incidents of accomplishments recorded herein were not put in word to intimate the author did anything extraordinary.

The focus of attention in this essay is directed toward individuals who have learning problems. In our nation, the school dropout rate is high. We may not agree on why this is the case, but we can probably agree that it is not advantageous to our society.

It is obvious that a college degree is not for everyone. That is not to say that those individuals who did not receive a college education were not capable of doing so. There are many, many people making a positive contribution to our society who have never set foot on a college campus. I congratulate you and certainly hold you in high regard. Thank you, and please keep on keeping on!

I hope this little book will encourage students to remain in school and do their best to graduate. Additionally, I hope it will encourage parents, grandparents, guardians, teachers, coaches, administrators, and others to extend a helping hand to the "slow learner" who is easily discouraged. Sometimes just a short word of praise, interest, understanding, and patience is enough.

In the final analysis it seems the greater responsibility falls to the primary helpers; that is, the parents and other adults at home. So stay the course and full speed ahead.

James

Acknowledgments

I wish to express my gratitude to Dr. Dallas D. Lutes, Dr. Otto Wasmer (deceased), and Dean M. Hayne Folk (deceased) for their encouragement during my undergraduate days at Louisiana Tech University, Ruston, Louisiana. Then to my major professor, Dr. Norman L. Horn, Louisiana State University, Baton Rouge, Louisiana, for without his help, understanding, and guidance, I would not have earned my PhD. Also, to Dr. I. L. Forbes (deceased), Louisiana State University, for his words of encouragement. I need to say a word of thanks to Dr. A. Wayne Owens, Ruston, Louisiana, for being in the right place at the right time. Also a special thanks to Dr. J. Colton Bradshaw, Mount Pleasant, Texas.

Additionally, thanks to Dr. Jeff H. Jenkins, retired professor, Western Kentucky University, Bowling Green,

Kentucky, and Dr. Jere M. McBride, retired Professor and Regional Director Louisiana State University Agricultural Center, Bossier City, Louisiana.

A most grateful thanks to my wife Donna, who never gave up in her support of me and my work. Also, to daughter Laura and son Jay, who have made our home a happy place to be.

Introduction

Following is a letter from my fourth-grade teacher at the end of summer school in 1948.

August 20, 1948

Dear Mr. and Mrs. White:

James is a friendly pupil who volunteers readily. There are times when he would rather talk about a matter than actually attack the job to be done.

James should be commended for his fine attitude, his regularity, and his promptness in doing extra work at one o'clock. We feel this has helped him to lessen the gap between himself and the major group. I am confident that James could "catch up" with the others if he would set himself to do extra work each evening next year. He does have ability. The more he does in arithmetic and reading—the more fun it will become.

We have been encouraging James to enunciate more distinctly. He often mumbles his words so that he can scarcely be understood.

This summer, James has improved in attention, in perseverance, and dependability.

Scholastically, James is a low average pupil. In arithmetic he has made commendable improvement in multiplication. He knows his combinations, but he is prone to make some slight error in longer problems. He has also gained in ability to read and solve thought problems. James has made gradual progress in reading. In oral reading he seems surer of himself and repeats himself less. He is quite accurate in comprehension. In written composition, James is careless. He often forgets his margin. He should break his ideas up into shorter sentences.

James knows the correct form for written work. Spelling is difficult for James because he does not hear sounds accurately. His written work often contains misspelled words. He usually misspells one word on weekly spelling tests. James knows how to form all his letters for cursive style of writing. He writes rapidly but needs to be more careful in letter formation and uniform slant.

Please know that we have appreciated your encouragement and cooperation in sending James back to school at one o'clock. We are sure that he has profited from this extra work.

Cordially yours,
Fourth Grade Teacher

This short story is written as a memorial to our grandson, Holden Yates, who was in a fatal auto accident at the age of sixteen on Sunday, April 18, 2004. Holden was a very special member of our family and had been diagnosed with dyslexia and attention deficit disorder (ADD). On numerous nights, I watched my wife Donna, who was an outstanding high school chemistry, physics, and biology teacher, work with Holden, who tried his hardest to learn his lessons and do his homework. I had a complete understanding of what Holden was going through, and so often I wanted to hug him and tell him not to get discouraged and not to give up. He may have felt discouraged on several occasions, but not once did he ever give up.

I feel that ADD was also a problem for me in my younger years, although the condition did not receive much attention in the 1940s and '50s. My guess is that most teachers were not aware of these conditions, and I was looked upon as just a "slow learner" or one of those who was not very smart. The purpose of this manuscript is not to bring attention to Holden and me, but to help those youngsters who have ADD as well as the parents and grandparents who struggle to help their youngsters learn. Additionally, it may be of some benefit to teachers who have problems working with their "slow learners."

You know, the ones who are just not able to pay close attention, who often daydream, have difficulty spelling, adding, subtracting, dividing, and ever so often disturb the class and interfere with other students who are capable of learning at a faster rate. Administrators should not be left out since they often have to solve/manage problems of discipline with some of these students.

I assume, for the most part, that the general public does not notice this type of person. Often the ADD, dyslexic individual just blends in and hopes he or she will not attract too much attention so the secret is not revealed. In my opinion, it is something like being a member of a private club, and you are the only member.

It is also my desire to pay tribute to Holden, who was always upbeat, happy, and more than willing to help others along the way. He was never argumentative or disagreeable, and if people were about to have a confrontation, he tried to head it off. He was often heard to say "peace easy" in his attempt to neutralize an argument. There is a memorial on the front lawn of his high school that has his name, dates, and "Peace Easy" inscribed on its face. God bless you, Holden. This is for you.

And to all those ADD, dyslexic people out there, please don't give up. You have a place, a purpose, and you do have gifts that will be of much use to others. Keep it simple, pay attention, and never give up. Peace easy.

1

Grammar School

Believe me when I say I know what it is like to feel you have no place to fit. I am without a niche and often feel I do not belong or maybe not even wanted. I listen but just do not understand. It seems I cannot hear fast enough. I know that sounds odd, but that was how I felt. *What was that word she used? I wish they would not talk so fast.* I can hear, but I am not able to understand. Later in life, I learned I did not, and still do not, hear syllables very well. And when several people are talking, I don't understand anybody. When my wife and I were dating and went to a movie, she usually spent much of the time telling me what was being said. I remember wondering how I could hear a duck quack in the distance or the splash of a fish jumping in the bayou but not hear and understand what was being said in a movie.

In the first grade, I was able to read, but much more slowly than most of my classmates. I was often asked to sit by myself or with a student teacher at another table and try to read. The first-grade room was large, with high ceilings and tall windows. I don't remember much about the first grade, except it was not much fun when I was asked to read out loud during reading period. I loved my first-grade teacher, who was a very kind and gentle lady. I know she did all she could to help me learn.

By the time I reached the third grade, I had begun to realize something was wrong with my ability to learn. It was also when I began to know school was going to be difficult for me. I am sure my parents were greatly concerned with my poor grades and my inability to master books. And I am sure the teachers were looking at me and wondering how I would ever get a formal education.

By the eighth grade, I think it became obvious to all the teachers that I was at the bottom of my class. I was one of the few who had to attend summer school. I do not remember any of my classmates who had to do that, although I am sure there were a few. It was a most difficult time for me. My arithmetic skills were virtually zero. I remember the large arithmetic book, and in the front was a bar graph that illustrated how well the student did with each lesson. A bar that went to the top indicated a perfect score for that lesson. It was all I could do to get my bars a third of the way up. I remember how embarrassed it made me feel to open the book to that page. I made every effort to hide it from fellow classmates.

But I must admit not one classmate or teacher ever made me feel dumb or that I did not belong. Those feelings I gave to myself. Nobody ever teased me about how slow I was at learning. I can remember thinking how smart all the girls were and, for many years, thought all girls were smarter than all boys. And I remember wondering how many of my buddies could do math, spell, and read at a rapid rate.

The best part of my grammar school days was recess. The boys often played a game called "hat ball," which was as much fun as baseball, football, or soccer. Each boy would dig a hole big enough to hold a tennis ball. We would stand in a circle around the holes while a fellow player would roll the ball toward the holes. If the ball ended up in your hole, all the players would scatter while you retrieved the ball and chased somebody down and hit him with it. If you missed, a wooden peg was placed in your hole. Three such pegs sent you before the firing squad, where each member threw the ball at your rear end from a distance of about fifteen feet. Some of the boys could really hum that old tennis ball, and often, a poor player would return to class with big red spots on his rump. Of course, it was all in fun, and I cannot remember anyone getting angry.

We often played football during recess in a small grassy spot just outside the principal's office. After sides were chosen before one particular game, Harry announced he was going to kick off. But to his surprise, I said it was my turn. When push came to shove, we ended up on the ground, and the game proceeded without either of us in the lineup. Harry was bigger than I and had my nose in the dirt when our principal, Mr. Vining, caught us by the necks and directed us to his office. Actually, I was glad to see him intervene, since Harry was about to really hurt me. After a serious talking to, he allowed us to return to our game. Harry and I were still good friends. We just had a minor problem as to who should kick off. It was also nice of Mr. Vining not to contact our parents, which made Harry and me most happy.

Our eighth-grade teacher told us she was planning to take the class on a trip to south Louisiana at the end of our school year. I am not sure how the girls felt about that, but the boys were excited. On the first night out, however, some of us boys almost got put on a bus and sent home. Someone had brought a deck of cards and suggested we have a game of strip poker in our room. We had food left over from lunches packed by our parents for the first day out. So we got in a circle and began to eat and play. As you can guess, we got louder as the game progressed. We also discarded chicken bones on the floor outside the little circle. When our teacher walked in to check out the noise and saw half-nude bodies and chicken bones, she neither laughed nor smiled. Well, after much begging, pleading, and promising to be really good, she forgave us, and we were able to remain with the rest of the group and not be sent home. She also did not tell our parents. That was a blessing; yes, a really good blessing.

The biggest scare I had during my grammar school days was when I got run over by a speeding log truck while riding my bike in front of my house. I was hit from behind and somehow fell on top of the bike. We all skidded to a halt, with the truck's back tires on top of my bike and about a foot from my head. I can still see those big treads if I allow myself to do so. My only injury was a scratch on my left elbow. Needless to say, that ended my bicycle-riding career.

All things considered, my grammar school days were good for me. I entered the ninth grade thinking I had been set free from some type of bondage I did not understand. There were about thirty members of my grammar school class and most of us went from the first to the eighth grade together. The friendships formed have lasted a lifetime. We all entered a high school with about six hundred students, so it was easy to understand why we felt as though we had been set free. Peace easy.

2

High School

My greatest fear as I entered high school was not of failure in my coursework but of being locked in a hall locker. I was a little guy, standing five foot two and weighing around one hundred pounds. I knew I would fit into one of those dark, ugly lockers. Sure enough, I got locked in one near my homeroom. A nice lady heard the screams and let me out. I will never forget the experience. I do not know who the boys were who did that bad deed. All I remember is they were bigger, and it apparently took very little effort to carry out their mission.

Another fear I had was being put into the big washer downstairs, where the athletic clothing was washed. That never happened, but I remember looking at that big washer with fear in my heart.

Of course, my fear was misplaced. Needless to say, my freshman year did not include any academic accomplishment. Frankly, it was a major disaster for me in math and English. My other courses were not much better. But there was one small glimmer of light. I went out for the varsity baseball team, and it appeared I had a chance to play third base. All else drifted off to some far off place where grades and academic accomplishment were not of much value. However, in practice one afternoon, I bent over for a grounder and could not get back into the standing position. The coach helped me over to the dugout where he left me in much pain and agony. I could see my entire world falling in around me, and I was most sad. A few days later our family physician, Dr. Marvin, gave the word to Dad and me that I would have to go into a back-brace immediately and for an extended period of time. No physical exercise, baseball, football, basketball, or track. I was to sleep on boards and not bend my back. It seems I had grown seven or eight inches in a short period of time and my vertebrae in my lower back had been pulled apart, resulting in a pinched nerve.

So there I was—unable to prove myself in athletics and unable to make good grades either. What a loser, and my freshman year was about to end. I could still hunt and fish without much pain. Thus, I placed a great deal of emphasis on those two hobbies. I had always been willing to fish and hunt as often as my Dad could take me. Also, I developed an interest in motorcycles and pickup trucks. These activities helped me to manage my inability to study and learn.

My coursework was not very interesting since it was difficult for me to understand and learn the subject matter. I was simply not interested in anything associated with the art of studying and learning. I do not remember reading any book that I was not required to read. It took a long time for me to read a book, and often I would have to read a paragraph three or four times before moving to the next.

For all practical purposes, they could have written my math, English, history, and science text in Russian.

Fractions—never mind! I remember being concerned about what was going to happen to me. There I was, unable to learn and in a stinking back brace. My mother had some body powder she used, and I would rub that stuff into the leather that covered the steel brace in an attempt to help control the odor. To this day, I do not like the smell of that powder.

I know the teachers were wondering what they were going to do with me. And for sure my parents were concerned. But somehow I was able to hang on and make just good enough grades to pass. Truly, by the end of my sophomore year, I had just about lost all interest in school, learning, and anything that had to do with academic achievement.

Thank goodness I was able to get dates and most girls did not mind being seen with me in public places and at dances. When my junior year started, I had a girlfriend, and Dr. Marvin said I could take off the brace, but he would allow only a limited amount of physical activity since I was in a weakened condition. I talked my parents into allowing me to go out for the basketball team, and

I was fortunate enough to make the traveling squad as a regular member of the second team. It was great fun, but it hurt. I never told my parents or anybody else for that matter, but many times after a game I would get in bed feeling like my back would break. I also was unable to bend over and wash my face the next morning. But playing basketball was something I could do at school other than learn, and it gave me a feeling of worth. Hunting, fishing, motorcycles, and trucks were not school-oriented activities.

Our junior class decided to have a play, and I was asked to be a member and actually have a leading part. I accepted, and while I played a major role, I did not utter a single word. I was some sort of villain that ran in, scared everybody, and then ran out. I think they called me Mr. Midnight. Since that time I have wondered why I was selected to play the Mr. Midnight part. However, as a result of being Mr. Midnight, I learned play acting would not be the career for me. I could not memorize lines anyway because of my inability to learn.

My junior year, as my freshman and sophomore years, was an academic disaster. However, I was having a huge amount of fun playing basketball, and with all my other activities, life had many rewards. At that point in time, as in the past, I did not fully realize how important it was that I learn how to learn. But I ask you, how do you learn how to learn when you don't know how to learn in the first place? I remember talking with Charlie, a close friend and classmate. He suggested we go live on the river after high school and become commercial fishermen. I thought that sounded good, but I wondered why he would want to do such a thing because he was, and still is, a highly intelligent person. I must say that the thought of living on the river, in the woods, and to come and go as I pleased did sound pretty good at that time in my life.

The summer between my junior and senior year, a cousin and I took my truck with my motorcycle in the back and went to work for an uncle in South Louisiana who was building a home. Boy, did we ever have ourselves a summer full of fun and work. We were on the job from sunup to sundown, and we went out on dates just about every night. When you are young, you are able to live that way and think nothing of it. High school was far, far away. Academic endeavors were not part of the table conversation. Life was simple and good for my cousin Roger and me. But the summer came to a close, and we had to make plans to go back home to North Louisiana. However, I managed to talk with my Uncle Tony about the possibility of getting a job at the local paper mill. He gave me a stern look and said he could get me put on extra-board, and I would probably work on the box line. The pay would not be very much, but to a person like myself who could not learn, it sounded pretty good. He told me, "You go back home and go to college. This paper mill job does not have much future, but if that is what you want to do, I'll help you all I can."

I came home to my senior year in high school confused because my uncle said I should go to college. I often wondered if he knew about my learning problem and was just trying to convince me I was college material. Perhaps he saw something in me that I and others could not see. Something told him that maybe James could learn and did have academic ability. But I still had to get through my senior year.

We had a new basketball coach, and as a result of his coaching ability, our team went to the state finals. We came home after our first game, but it was a good starting year for him. He was a great coach and a fine man. Also, I signed up to take journalism and was the sports editor for our school paper. I greatly enjoyed covering all the sporting events and considered making journalism a lifetime career, but I lost interest post-graduation. Again, I went out for baseball, made the team at third base, played one game, and then dropped out in order to place more emphasis upon my fishing interest. Baseball was in direct conflict with the spring spawning of bass and bream. I also sang in the senior choir and mixed quartet and won some sort of medal at a singing event held at the local college. I ran track, but only in the second heat, where I managed to win the 220 yard dash at one local meet. In the meantime, I learned how to play the guitar, in a simple sort of way, but found out it provided much entertainment for me and did not require reading, spelling, math, or science. Additionally, somewhere along the way, I picked up a harmonica and to my surprise, I could play it better than I could play my guitar. Some time later, my dad told me his sister Mabel was a good harmonica player, and it seemed to have come naturally to her as well.

During my senior year, my brother-in-law Joe and I developed an interest in building eight-foot-long hydroplanes that would accommodate a ten horsepower outboard motor. So now my interest included speedboats. Anything but academic pursuits! Anything to take my mind away from that ever-present void in my life—my inability to learn. I should point out that I managed to flip that hydroplane in the middle of a large private lake outside of town. Fortunately, air got trapped in the bow, and I held on until help arrived. And no, I was not wearing a life vest. And yes, that ended my speedboat racing career.

My senior year, like the previous years, was an academic disaster. I feel sure my homeroom teacher looked upon me as one of those kids who would never attend any college, anywhere. She had watched me grow and develop for four long years, and I do not blame her if she was glad to be rid of me.

By then I was fully convinced that I needed to get out of town, and I considered entering a branch of the service. I looked into the Navy and Air Force and went home and announced my plans to my mother, who immediately threw a fit. She told me that every member of her family, which included eight siblings, had attended college and that I would also attend college. For her and her brothers and sisters to attend college was a very special accomplishment since they were raised on a 160-acre farm in the middle of nowhere. And when my mother put her foot down, that was it. The show was over. No ifs, ands, or buts—just you do it. I am sure she was about at her wit's end with her one and only son, who had avoided academic achievement for several years at that point. I can remember wondering if she knew about my learning problem. Perhaps, just maybe, she did not know. On the other hand, she may have thought I could go to college and even graduate. I thought, *I will go, but it sure will not be for long.* I had spelling problems and I was a slow reader, not to mention my attitude toward math, English, and science. And besides all that, I was not sure what I wanted to be in life. I knew journalism and play acting were out. When I was younger I thought I might become a preacher. My dad was a preacher, and I guess I identified with him and what he did. Since I viewed my dad as being a perfect person, I knew I could never fill his shoes. I was far too rowdy to ever be a man of the cloth, so preaching was deleted from my list

Now I really had a problem. What was I going to do when I got kicked out of college? It was going to upset my parents when they realized that their son was not very smart and unable to earn a living. My older sister Rose had gone through high school with all good grades and was now in college, married, and doing right well. Then along came James. Mercy, what a mess I had on my hands. My attempt to run away had failed! There was always the river and commercial fishing and living in the woods where I would be hard to find. But I did not want to hurt my parents by living in the woods and not telling them where I could be found.

That summer I worked again in construction. I really liked it and enjoyed all the people associated with the building industry. I loved being a carpenter's helper and watching the carpenters put things together. When I cut and put things together, it was never square, not the right length, bent, or in one way or another not right. I also liked being a brick mason's helper and thought I would like to enter that trade. My good friend J. D., who was a brick mason, told me, "James, it is hot in the summer and cold in the winter. You had better go on to college." He drove a nice car, and I remember thinking, *But you have such a nice car.* My priorities were still somewhat mixed up.

Since my dad was a preacher, I did not have a family business to take over. Our family did not own any land, so it was not possible for me to work the soil. We did not have any extra money for me to invest in any type of venture, so I was being backed into a corner. I have often wondered if God was not involved in all of that. If I were being pushed in a direction in which I did not think I was capable of going. I do not like to use the "d" word, but I had every reason to think I could be a little on the dumb side.

From the get-go, I never once excelled in academic matters. From the first grade through high school, not one academic accomplishment. Here I was, at the eleventh hour, getting ready to enter the college ranks. No reason for me to think I would ever graduate. No reason to think I was capable of earning a bachelor's degree. No reason to think I could do much of anything at the college level since I could not learn, I could not stay focused, and I did not have any idea as to what I wanted to become in life. If you have been there, then you know the feeling. If you have not been there, *you do not have a clue.*

The summer following high school graduation found me in the construction business once more. The heat never bothered me, and I enjoyed the freedom from the classroom and books. In the back of my mind there lingered an empty feeling about college and how I would manage. All the boys in my little group were going to college, and they just assumed I had made appropriate plans. But no plans were made since I had no idea what plans should and needed to be made. I had saved my money and lived at home. My parents still provided food, clothing, and shelter, and there was a charge account down at the gas station and hardware store. I loved the hardware store since it also sold sporting equipment and supplies. My fishing and hunting activities had expanded, and my buddies and I had several duck blinds on different lakes around North and Central Louisiana. I had also managed to purchase a boat (my dad paid half the price) and a used ten-horsepower outboard motor. I had a boat rack on my truck, a place to attach my motor, extra gas tanks, a tent, and all the other stuff necessary to stay in the swamp for an extended period of time. It was a great life, and it did not require me to read, spell, or do math and science. Regardless, when the thought of college surfaced in my mind, it brought with it a feeling of hopelessness. I began to wonder what my friends would think when I got kicked out of college.

That summer flew by in a flash, and before I realized what had taken place, I was on the college campus getting ready to register for classes. I remember really being impressed with courses being taught in different buildings on the campus and having time off between classes. Peace easy.

3

College Undergraduate (Phase I)

This part of my life story is still embarrassing to think about, but it happened, was important, and must be included. I did not know what a major was, or even how to get registered. Acceptance to college was a given so I sent in the application forms and went to registration. When I entered the gymnasium where registration was held I looked around in total amazement. This was the same gym where I had played several high school tournament basketball games. I looked at the goal where I once had the opportunity to be the hero. We were playing a team we had very seldom beaten, and we were one point behind. In the last second of play, I went up for a jump shot but was fouled and consequently missed the basket. The clock had run out of time when I went to the foul line. The gym was full of fans. It got quiet in our section. I missed my first shot, and when I glanced at the bench, I saw the coach hang his head. *That is okay, White,* I told myself. *Just relax, shoot your second shot, tie the score, and we can go into overtime.* Boom! I missed my second shot, and the game was over.

Now back to this major thing. I sat down at the first table I came to and looked around. The departments were arranged in alphabetical order, so the table had coursework for those students who planned to pursue art as a career. The lady at the table was very nice, and I think she knew my parents, and she was kind enough to talk with me about what major I would like to pursue. After a short while I felt like I would like to major in art, and I signed up to be an art major. I immediately felt better since a big decision had been made, and I knew what it was I was to be in life. I thought, *That was kind of easy,* and I was actually excited about this big-time accomplishment. Of course, I did not tell the nice lady about my inability to learn, for I knew she would find out soon enough

It is difficult to understand how and why some events in life play out. Many of us in our older years shake our heads, smile, and wonder when thinking of the past. After I had selected my major, I ran into my old friend, Middleton. We met in the first grade, liked each other, and have remained friends to this day. However, the influence we exerted on one another was not always positive. But guess what? Middleton had also decided to major in art. What more could I ask for? If the nice lady had realized what she had just allowed to take place, her hair would have turned gray overnight.

Frankly, I am not able to remember much about that first semester. I do remember that all freshmen had to take an entrance exam that would indicate if they would graduate or maybe what field of study they should be in. The test is just a blur in my memory because as I was entering the building to take the exam, I ran into a fishing buddy who told me the bass were really hitting down at the camp. He also told me to hurry up so we could get there early enough to catch our limits. I was so excited over the news that I did not bother to read most of the questions. Since it was a multiple-choice exam, all I had to do was put down the marks. I was one of the first to finish. It really did not matter since my college career would be over at the end of the year anyway.

We had a great trip, and while we did not limit out, we caught several good bass. I later learned that the score I made on that exam indicated I would flunk out of college the first year. So I was off to a great beginning. College was going to be fun. My first semester was a disaster, and I guess the F in Art Appreciation was probably the most hurtful event of this new career of mine. The course was taught at eight o'clock on Saturday morning, and it was most difficult for me to stay focused. Somehow, I managed to pass my other courses, not with good grades, but I passed. It should be pointed out that I dropped botany before I flunked and that unacceptable performance did not count against my grade point average.

The second semester was just as good. Once again, the love of fishing interfered with my studies. I had to turn in a big art laboratory assignment, but on my way with it in hand, I ran into a fishing buddy (not Middleton), and you know the rest of the story. We went to the camp and fished all day. The next day I had to turn in the assignment late and face the nice lady I had met during registration. She was also the department head and not one to put up with a slacker. She asked why I was late, and since I have never been a good liar, I told her that I had gone fishing. She had put up with me for a year now, waiting for me to make a turnaround. Enough was enough, and I did not blame her for telling me how she felt about my first year's performance. Of course, I said I did not want to be an artist anyway, and I would be changing my major to something else. She told me I should reconsider that. But it kind of hurt my feelings and caused some irritation that she was being so honest with me. I went back later that day and apologized for not accepting her criticism with an open heart. She let me know that she thought well of me and that there were no hard feelings, but she also suggested I might want to consider another career.

I am not sure why, but Middleton changed his major to bacteriology very soon thereafter. Following graduation he, his wife, and family moved to Florida, where he had a rewarding career as a professional bacteriologist. After retirement, he developed an interest in oil painting. Now Middleton goes by Milt and is a well-known, highly successful oil painter in that state using marsh scenes as his subject.

Once again, my summer was spent in construction, and I was able to save enough money to stay in college another year. I had no idea what I should do about a new major. My inability to learn was causing a serious problem. I did not know how to take notes, and some of the courses were really difficult for me, especially botany. All those big names, and the professor expected me to be able to spell them letter perfect. How was it possible for a person like me to be able to pass a course like that? My answer to myself was a downer. I would never be able to pass such a course.

I do not know what prompted me to make the decision to major in business. I knew absolutely nothing about business, never worked in a business other than as a common laborer in construction, and did not have any money to start up a business. It was during the fall semester when a student friend asked me when I planned to take accounting. I asked him what accounting was, and when he told me I realized that I may be in the wrong field. Maybe I should not be a businessman after all. It was later that semester that I got up and walked out of my business math class because I was tired of trying to figure out how to work all those dang problems. My homework was in awful shape, and I told the lady teaching the class just to send me my F because I was done with that class. She sure had an odd look on her face when I walked out.

Without doubt I was getting in deeper and deeper. Once again, I felt as though I was being backed into a corner and there was no way out. I knew of no place to go to find anybody who could help me. Or maybe I just did not want any help. Maybe I felt a person like me, who could not learn, could not be helped. At the beginning of my junior year, I went by the business office and asked the lady what I would have to take in the fall semester in order to stay in the School of Business. She told me I had to take eighteen hours and make a B average. The worst was now face to face with me. I was not sure if I had made a B at that point in my college career. The three-point system was in place at that time, and I had managed to earn a 0.8. The truth was about to be announced to the world, and there was no place for me to hide. I remember standing at that desk and wondering how I would solve this problem. Maybe there was something else I could major in and avoid this impending disaster.

It is strange how things seem to work out. I have read in several books that many people do not believe in coincidences. That there is a master plan and all of us have a gift that can be used to help others along the way.

The business office was directly across the hall from the bacteriology laboratory, and as I turned out of the business office, I looked through an open door and saw my lifelong friend and fishing buddy Wayne. Wayne was not the one I got in so much trouble with when I skipped out and went fishing those two critical times. Our eyes met, and he motioned for me to come on in. He was alone in the lab with the bacteriology professor, and they were transferring bacteria from one test tube to another. This is simply known as making transfers. I remember seeing the red hot inoculating needle cool down as Wayne skillfully touched the bacteria in the first tube and placed them on fresh growth medium in the second tube. I later learned this procedure had to be carried out regularly or the bacteria may slow down in their growth rate. All stock cultures had to be maintained in a fresh state so they could be used by students in the laboratory and perform as they should perform. I was really impressed with Wayne not only because he could make transfers but also because he was a teaching assistant in the lab. He wore a white laboratory coat, and I just sat in awe. Wayne is now a highly respected physician in our community and still a very close friend. Peace easy.

4

College Undergraduate: The Turnaround (Phase II)

Wayne introduced me to the bacteriology professor, and to my surprise, he was actually a real, living human being. I had never spoken to such a person and had considered most college professors as the enemy. Also, it occurred to me that it might be possible for this man to look inside me and identify my learning disability. I think I was somewhat nervous being placed in a position where I had to carry on a conversation with a PhD.

Wayne asked me how things had been going since he had not seen me in a while. I told him of my little problem with the School of Business and that my college career was in its final stages of development. In all probability I would not register for the fall semester and begin my junior year. It was over. It hurt me to make that public announcement, especially in the presence of a PhD whom I had just met.

Wayne said to me, "James, you don't need to drop out of school. You love the out of doors, why don't you major in Wildlife Conservation and Management?" I was shocked at that suggestion. I had not considered wildlife management, and it sounded pretty good to me. I got excited, but then I remembered about my inability to learn, and botany was one of the first courses to be taken. My response was thank you, but no thanks, for I will never be able to pass botany. They both smiled and agreed that passing botany would not be a problem for me. I assured them it would be a problem. Then the professor made a statement I shall remember all of my life, for it stopped me in my tracks. He said, "If you will give it a try, I will teach you how to study and learn."

I had just met this man, and he was willing to help me learn. This I could not believe was possible. My academic trail, at best, was unacceptable. I then said that my grades were too poor and that I would not be allowed to transfer into the School of Agriculture and Forestry. They responded by saying that we would let the dean of the school pass judgment, and they escorted me to the dean's office. The dean was a most kind and gentle man and one of those rare individuals who loved people. After we talked for a while, he told me I could transfer into his school, but on the condition that I made my grades the first semester. It had been placed in my lap—the opportunity to make a turnaround and maybe actually graduate from college.

A lifelong friend and a PhD college professor had taken the time and cared enough to point me in the right direction and then give me a shove. Also, a college dean had taken the time to listen to a stammering student try to explain his life of academic failure and then, with a smile, accepted me, the slow learner, into the fold.

I ask, was all this coincidence? I think not. Peace easy.

5

College Undergraduate: Donna (Phase III)

The opportunity was there, right directly in front of me. But could I overcome this learning problem that had been holding me back since the first grade? Would I be able to learn how to learn, and do I, James White, actually have a special gift, or gifts, that may be of some use to others? Without doubt, I sheltered many fears of failure. Up to this point, my fear was failing the expectations of my parents; now the list had been enlarged to include my lifelong friend Wayne, the bacteriology professor, and the awesome dean. The fear of being locked up in a dark hall locker had taken a back seat, and now I faced the real fear of flunking out of college. I was standing on thin ice, and the commercial fishing idea always loomed in the back of my mind. But that would be running away from something I had never been able to understand and manage. Why was I not able to learn as others were able to learn? Would that always be with me? As I approach seventy-six years of age, I am able to say yes, I will always be a slow learner, but that does not mean that I do not have the capability to learn. I have learned that if I want to learn about something, it will take longer for me to accomplish that goal as compared with an individual who has been blessed with a faster learning capacity. When I left the office of the awesome dean, I had mixed emotions.

I was not sure I really wanted to be in Wildlife Management. I was not sure I would actually be able to stay focused long enough to master any academic challenge that crossed my path. I was especially concerned about botany, which had already defeated me once. The thought of that failure inflicted a sharp pain in my innermost self.

The road to graduation seemed to be all uphill, full of curves, rocks, and storms. But now, at least there was some hope. If I looked real hard I could see a dim light at the end of a long, long tunnel. The summer prior to my junior year again found me as a construction worker. But for some reason, for the first time in my life, I realized I may not return to construction work as a source of income. Although I enjoyed that way of earning a living, I realized its departure would result in my life going in another direction. That also bothered me, since it was the only type of work I could do and it gave me a most comfortable feeling. It also made me feel secure, and it still does, though even now I am unable to build anything square and level. But I like to try, and I like to be around people who have elected to make a career out of building things.

That summer, I also met a girl named Donna. I had a date with one of her best friends and Donna had a date with one of my best friends. We were double dating, as we called it in the 1950s. I think people double dated because most kids did not have ready access to a nice automobile. We did not know it at the time, but the following summer, Donna and I would be married.

Fall registration came in like a fast running storm, and my schedule included General Bacteriology and General Botany. There was fear, agony, and pain within my poor mind and body. I was going to have to make transfers and learn how to spell some very big words that I could not begin to even pronounce. I had no idea people had to work so hard to make good grades.

Donna's major was zoology, and she was training to become a medical laboratory technologist. Since she was a member of the Department of Zoology and I was a member of the Department of Botany and Bacteriology, our paths crossed early in the semester. Naturally, I asked her for a date, and to my surprise, she accepted. Because it was a Sunday night date we went to church service, then out for a hamburger, and then back to her dormitory. As I recall, she and all of the other girls had to be in by eight o'clock in the evening.

In a very short period of time, we were dating on a regular basis. Our dates were not like anything I had ever experienced because instead of going to a movie or going to get a hamburger, we ended up at my house studying. She studied every night and this was difficult for me to understand. I did not realize that smart people, those who were not considered to be slow learners, had to study in order to make good grades. She worked really hard and took school work seriously. Of course, she graduated cum laude and also picked up the French Governmental Award along the way. But this was my first semester at my new life, and all this studying and book work went against everything I had ever done.

The PhD bacteriologist had placed a strict study requirement upon me and now Donna was doing the same thing. It was almost more than I could bear. There were many stressful moments, and I was not sure I had made the right decision. I remember the first night I went to the library. Donna announced that afternoon, "Tonight we need to go to the library." At that time in my college career, I had not been in the library and was not even sure of its location. It made a lasting impression on me. I remember the door where we entered and looking at all those books. I was surprised to see that there were other students there studying. It was very still and quiet. Donna selected a table, and we began our studies. Within ten or fifteen minutes, I thought I would jump out of my skin. Between the quietness and the hum of fluorescent lights, I was giving the commercial fishing another thought or two. But some unseen force gave me the patience to sit, read, and study my lessons. When our studies were complete, it was time for Donna to return to her dormitory. I think the girls were allowed to stay out until nine on weeknights. Man, what an exciting night out, and I knew there would be many more like this one if I stayed on course.

But I was learning how to learn. I actually took notes in every class. That was something I had never been able to do. Before, when I went to class, I just sat and listened and did not once give note-taking much value. When I looked around and paid some attention to other class members, I saw that they were taking notes. I came to realize that note-taking was very important and helpful since notes often contained information not found in the textbook, and the professor felt that what he said during lecture was important enough to be placed upon the next exam. I also attended all class meetings, was never late, and did my homework on time. Probably one of the most difficult things to do was establish a new list of priorities, with fishing, hunting, pickup trucks, speed boats, motorcycles, and hanging out with friends all toward the bottom of the list.

At the end of the first semester of my new life, I received two rewards: An A in General Bacteriology and an A in General Botany. Apparently all those long hours of hard work over the books and notes had paid off. For the first time in my life, that dim light at the end of that long, long, tunnel got just a little brighter. I had indeed learned how to learn. I also realized that it would not be easy for me, but if I did not give up, if I studied every night, if I put first things first, then goals I once believed to be unattainable would be attainable. Thank you, Wayne; thank you, PhD bacteriologist; thank you, awesome dean; thank you, Donna; and thank you, Jesus.

I knew I was going to graduate. What I did not know was how hard it was going to be, how long it was going to take, and how much money it required. I was so happy over my first semester results that it was impossible for me to see beyond the end of my nose. Toward the end of the second semester of my new life, I met and began to know a PhD in the department who was in charge of the General Botany Laboratory sections. He asked if I would consider being a botany laboratory assistant starting the following fall and change my major to botany. Now, that was almost too much for this slow learner who had to drop botany the first time around. Unbelievable! Absolutely unbelievable! Impossible! Out of sight! Am I a witness to a miracle? Is this really happening to me? Although the only thing I had ever taught was Sunday school to some preteens, I thought teaching sounded like fun.

Another big decision was made that semester. I asked Donna if she would marry me and try to make a go of it together. I guess I took an unfair advantage of her and later wondered if she has held that against me. We went to the state fair together, and I talked her into taking a ride on a large Ferris wheel. She did not like high places. It just so happened that the wheel stopped while we were at the top, so I began to swing back and forth. Of course she was about to have a spasm, and that is when I told her I would stop the rocking if she would marry me. Without any hesitation, she said yes and to get her off that thing. Neither of us had the slightest notion what it was I wanted to do with my life and that made me question her judgment. Regardless, we were married on July 13, 1957, and fifty-four years later we are still together.

The summer of '57 once again found me as a member of a construction crew. I needed some quick money so Donna and I would not starve. That fall semester, which was the third semester of my new life, was very busy. Donna worked as the secretary for the Zoology Department and was also on weekend call at our local hospital. I taught labs, and our total monthly income was ninety dollars. We lived close to my parents, and Mother fed us every day at noon. We provided our own breakfast and supper, and my dad paid our monthly rent, which was thirty dollars. But once again, my hard work with the books was paying big dividends. For the first time in my new life situation, I made more As than Bs and the light at the end of the long, long tunnel was now even brighter.

The PhD who asked me to teach labs encouraged me to conduct an independent research project. I had developed to the point where I could sit in the presence of these professors and not have a nervous rigor. I don't think they ever looked upon me as a slow learner but as a person with capability. They seemed to think I was academically qualified and also capable of conducting an independent research project. This was almost more than I could stand. The project was carried out during that winter and finalized in early March. Then I received another shocker when I was asked to present my research at the state academy annual meeting, which was being held at another college in the central area of our state. After my presentation, I met and talked with people who were interested in my work, and one professor from that college, I believe he was the head of the department, expressed an interest in my future plans. Donna accompanied me to the meeting, and we returned home with great expectations and hope.

When we got our feet on the ground, I guess I received the greatest of all shockers. Just three semesters back this slow learner had been on the skids, on his way out of college. The PhD in charge of the labs called me into his office and told me he wanted me to go to graduate school. I had heard about graduate school, but I did not know what or where it was. My focus was upon the undergraduate degree and trying to find a job somewhere that would keep Donna and me out of the poorhouse. I learned there were two degrees one could earn at graduate school. One was a masters and the other was a doctorate or PhD. My blood ran cold. I could never, ever, earn a degree that would place me on the same level as these two professors who were so intelligent, so learned, so well-informed. Both of them had taken on a hero status in my life. I wanted to say, "No sir, I cannot do that. You see, I am not very smart, and it takes so long for me to learn anything. What takes Donna an hour to learn takes me three hours." That "slow learner" brand was still burning, and it was impossible for me to ignore its deep-seated meaning. But I could not make myself say, "No sir." I'm not sure why, and I guess deep down I wanted to pattern my life after these two gentlemen and that awesome dean. But to imagine that someday someone may refer to me as Doctor White or "Doc" was one of those unattainable goals.

I talked with Donna, and she felt I should give it a try. It was too late for me to consider a career as a commercial fisherman over on the river, and I knew I would never go into play acting or journalism. So, what the heck: go for it. If I flunked out of graduate school, it would not matter because it was in some far off place and nobody back home would ever know.

My last summer at the undergraduate level was occupied with coursework so I could enter graduate school the following February. I took Ecology, Organic Chemistry, and Physics and often wished I was out on some construction job burning up in the heat. When I thought of what was ahead for me academically speaking, a knot would form in my stomach. Was I crazy? How did

I get into such a mess? The fear of being locked up in a dark hall locker seemed minor compared to the fear I now had. All of these people who had placed so much confidence in me, who had devoted their time and energy to help me make my grades and helped me learn how to learn, were expecting me to go all the way.

During that last semester, I sent in my application to the Graduate School of Louisiana State University, Baton Rouge, Louisiana. They accepted me but on probation for the first semester. When I read their letter, it totally destroyed all my desire to go. I made up my mind I would not go under those conditions, but Donna and the professors talked me into changing my mind. I had also been offered a botany teaching assistantship in the department, and I really did not want to turn it down. Once again, my grades were good and I made more As than Bs. That February, Donna and I graduated together, and as I pointed out earlier, she graduated cum laude. I did not graduate cum laude, but I did graduate with Departmental Honors; and for me that was a major accomplishment. Peace easy.

Undergraduate Study Tips

Before we enter the land of the Great Graduate School, I think it would be of some value to those who have a difficult time learning for me to list some the things that helped me to learn. Probably these should be termed learning tools, but since I still think of tools as hammers, saws, squares, and levels, I'll just say these are some of the things that helped me remain focused and eventually earn my undergraduate degree. Let me emphasize that it was not, and still is not, easy for me to learn. The necessity for me to have to work in order to learn will be a lifelong essential. Therefore, if I wish to learn about something, I must be willing to devote an appreciable amount of my time and energy to that endeavor, or I will not learn.

Here is an incomplete list of the things that helped me learn:

1. I studied by myself, not with a group of people. I sought help only to update and correct my notes.

2. I learned to take good notes and rewrote those notes as soon as possible. No later than that night. I rewrote them using black ink.

3. I looked at the teacher's face as much as possible. This seemed to help me keep my mind on what was being said.

4. When possible, I would sit where I could have a good view of the blackboard and professor. I could also hear better when I was close to the front.

5. I became a neat and orderly person. Neat in clothing and neat in note-taking and storage of books. I started a small library by not selling my textbooks.

6. I never allowed myself to get behind. I never missed a class or an exam, and I never was late for a class.

7. I never put myself in a position to have to do make-up work.

8. I tried to get plenty of sleep and eat properly.

9. I kept a dictionary on my desk at all times and still do.

10. I did not set unrealistic goals.

11. I did not slouch in my sitting or standing position. If I allowed myself to slouch, my focus would be lost and I would daydream.

12. When necessary, I sought help from a person I trusted and who was well qualified to lend assistance.

13. I avoided persons who were negative or who might ridicule others and me. Negative statements are very powerful and difficult to forget. Don't say them, and don't listen to them.

14. Although it was difficult, I learned never to put a hobby at the top of my list when I was trying to learn. I learned it was of utmost importance to become a responsible person, not only to myself but to all people.

15. It became obvious that I had to establish a strict schedule and stick to that schedule because it brought order to my life. For me to learn, everything had to be in order. I could not learn with the radio or TV on. Light classical, instrumental music was permissible, but not too loud.

16. I had to convince myself not to give up regardless of the situation.

It is my hope that this information will be useful to any person who finds learning difficult. It worked for me. However, having two professors who took an interest in me, an awesome dean who put the opportunity in my lap and being married to the right person were highly instrumental in helping me along the way. Donna has been a constant source of strength, and she never questioned my ability to learn. I also feel that my life has been under God's direction, but it was a long time before I was aware of that fact. Peace easy.

6

The Land of the Great Graduate
School (Phase IV)

In February, Donna and I packed up all our stuff
and headed off into the unknown, to the land of the
Great Graduate School where higher degrees could be
found. We moved into a small one bedroom, one bath
apartment near the school and came to the realization
that many new adjustments were necessary. Relocating
from a small college to LSU, which housed the Great
Graduate School, was most traumatic to say the least.
We were accustomed to having a yard with trees, grass,
shade, and privacy. All of that was a thing of the past,
as were the free noon meals at Mom and Dad's house.
Our lives would never be the same. We were in a land

where all was new and strange. Most of the people in this land to the south had never heard of our land to the north, and as far as I could determine, many were not particularly interested one way or the other.

It was not long before we met another couple, Jeff and Martha, who were also from a small, far off college. We were very poor and had no idea what we were about to go through for the next few years. The following semester we were joined by Jere Mac who, like Donna and me, came from the small college in the north. Jere Mac, Jeff, and I all majored in plant pathology and occupied the same office during our tenure at LSU. Had any of us had any idea about our future, I feel sure Jere Mac would have taken a job at the paper mill in his hometown, Jeff would have stayed on his dad's small farm, and I would have moved to the river and become a commercial fisherman. A bond was formed between us that has lasted for all these many years.

One thing that impressed me at this new level of learning was that all the professors were expected to conduct a well-planned research program, publish, and present papers at professional meetings. Many were excellent teachers and enjoyed being around graduate students, but most of their energy was directed toward research. To the best of my knowledge, the department head talked with each graduate student separately and suggested courses to take. Right up front we all said, "Yes sir, I think those are the courses I need. Thank you, sir, for taking time out of your busy schedule to give me this advice and direction." I will never forget that first semester Jeff and I found out what courses we would take. We made our separate visits and then returned to our office somewhat awestruck. We had been in the office of the department head and talked with him face to face and that only took place once each semester. It was a very scary thing for us to do since he had an international reputation and was highly respected for his many contributions to science. It was also rumored in the halls of the Great Graduate School that he had *total recall*. I had heard about *total recall* but never actually sat face to face with such an individual. It worried me because I had the feeling he could look inside me and see that I was a slow learner, and those old fears began to float to the surface. I wondered if I would ever reach a time in my life when that kind of thinking would not bother me.

Anyway, back to Jeff. When he returned to our office, I was sitting there wondering how things were going at the small college to the north. Jeff looked at me, frowned, and asked, "What is mycology?" Maybe that was the first time I had smiled since leaving my nest up north because I finally knew something a fast learner did not know! Jeff asked me that question fifty-one years ago, but I still remember, and it seems like it just happened yesterday. I actually knew something a fast learner did not know! I had taken General and Medical Mycology at the undergraduate level and had the jump on him. I asked why he needed to know, and he told me the department head down the hall told him he would have to take mycology, and he had never heard of mycology.

Another important aspect about my graduate school experience was the selection of a major professor and the type of research program available. Much care and attention was required in order that all involved would be on the same page. I could not have asked for a better major professor. He was a super-nice man with a great personality. His major field of research involved diseases of strawberry fruit, and he was also a fisherman. I love strawberries and fishing, and life was once again good.

For the most part, Jere Mac, Jeff, and I attended class during the day and also conducted research in the laboratory, greenhouse, or field. Nights were devoted to library research. We were required to take two seminars each semester. One of my undergraduate professors had warned me about seminar and somehow I managed to control my fear. It was not easy, since speaking before groups had not been one of my strong features. Big Seminar was held from three to five on Wednesday afternoon for two hours' credit and Little Seminar was from nine to ten on Friday morning for one hour of credit.

The topics and dates of presentation for Big Seminar were posted on the bulletin board down the hall next to the department head's door. For the most part, I could never remember any topic I was familiar with or knew anything about. I would simply close my eyes and take the one I touched. One semester I was late in my selection and only one topic was left. I later learned why.

Big Seminar usually required reviewing thirty-plus publications about the topic and the preparation of a multiple-page handout discussing the topic and listing all publications reviewed. All faculty and graduate students were expected to attend and could question the speaker at any moment during the presentation. If the speaker could not adequately answer a question, he then was required to revisit the library during the week and present the correct answer before the next seminar started. Additionally, the speaker was expected to furnish three cakes, made available in the coffee room, to be consumed prior to the presentation by those who were in attendance. I never ate any cake, which Donna had baked, prior to any of my presentations.

The first seminar Jeff and I attended, the presenter never got past the first page of his handout. There were so many questions from the professors that the topic was never really covered. Jeff and I went back to our office and sat there trembling. One thing was for sure; I was having second thoughts and ready to go home. So was Jeff. But then a light entered our office and it was one of the older, likable professors. He told us, "Boys, don't let that bother you. It will be all right. You just hang in there and do the best job you can do." The encouragement came just at the right time.

In Little Seminar we just had to review one paper in a critical sort of way, and all faculty and graduate students were not expected to attend. Also, there was no cake requirement and the stress level was much lower. I guess seminar was not so bad for me since I never made lower than an A in Big or Little Seminar, and I never had to revisit the library in order to properly answer a question. I had made up my mind to become a college professor and realized how important it was to present subject matter in a highly organized, professional manner. Seminar helped me to accomplish that goal.

I made my grades that first semester and was taken off probation. All of the things that helped me learn at the undergraduate level also helped me learn at the graduate level. It still seemed like a dream that I was able to stay in graduate school and make good grades. My research was progressing, and every so often my major professor would take me fishing. I could never feel comfortable in his presence due to my feeling of inferiority brought about by my inability to learn. The brand still burned and there was nothing I could do to stop that emotion. But he always treated me with respect even though I was a lowly graduate student. I was never sure if he was aware of my inability to learn; if he was, he was nice enough not to let me know. I thank you, sir.

During our first year in graduate school, Donna and I decided to start our family. Our first child, Laura Beth, was born, and our lives changed once again. We moved into a larger apartment with two bedrooms and close to the campus. Donna had been hired as the histopathology technician for the Department of Veterinary Science at LSU, and her salary made the move to a larger place possible.

But storm clouds were gathering, and I was sure lightning would strike, but not where or when. Jere Mac, Jeff, and I finished our coursework and research the same semester and, not thinking properly, we scheduled our oral and qualifying exams on different days of the same week. During this exam, the student is held responsible for his research, coursework, and anything else the committee wished to throw in. Jere Mac was first, Jeff second, and I was last. When Jere Mac returned to the office, he was pale and said they asked him questions he had no idea how to answer. Jeff and I listened and shook our heads. When Jeff returned from his exam, he had a similar story but somewhat worse, and I listened, shook, and wondered why I was putting myself through all this. By the time Friday arrived, I was a nervous wreck. I had great fear of a member of my committee, but when the exam started, he was not present. During my exam I was doing so well that the older professor (the one who gave Jeff and me needed encouragement) gave a nod of approval and left early. But when the professor I feared came in late, I went absolutely blank. The show was over and it was time to go home. I don't remember much after that, and the committee required that I take a written exam in addition to the oral. Later in my office, the older professor came in and asked me what had happened after he left. I told him, and he shook his head and said, "Just do the best you can do and don't worry." He did not submit any questions for me to address in the form of a written exam. Thank you again, sir.

At this stage in my graduate career, it appeared that the last act was about to be played. I did worry and felt maybe it was not for me to be a college professor and pattern my life after the professors back home and the awesome dean. The goal of PhD seemed unattainable. Even though I had been able to make twelve As and five Bs, I felt I was a total failure. Although the Great Graduate School was far away from the small college in the north, I had the feeling that all eyes were focused upon me and people were saying, "I told you so."

I took my written exam and apparently did a good job. My major professor came in the office a short time later and said I had passed and everything was in order for me to continue my studies and work toward the PhD as planned. He also consented to allow me to continue working under his guidance. I was most grateful, and I thank you, sir. The light at the end of the tunnel got a little bit brighter.

Later, my major professor asked if I would like to present my research at the national meeting of our professional society. I was totally surprised that my major professor would allow my work to be made public at such an event. Of course I said yes, and he then told me that the meeting was to be in Wisconsin. I had heard about Wisconsin from the PhD bacteriologist who also told me of a famous university within its borders. We drove to the meeting in a university owned automobile, and the trip seemed to take forever. Regardless, the rewards were too great to allow any discomfort to interfere with this event. I remember very little about my presentation except there was a large number of professionals attending that session. During the break after my presentation, two or three scientists expressed interest in my work. Eventually, my major professor published my research in our professional journal and listed me as the senior author. Once again, I thank you, sir. That publication was later cited in a book authored by a well-known plant pathologist/physiologist.

It sure was strange, but a short while back I was about to flunk out of college, and there I was in Wisconsin discussing my research with learned scientists. As a result, I decided I would like to continue this research for my dissertation and my major professor approved.

In order to graduate with the PhD, it was necessary for all graduate students to pass two foreign language exams. For those in our area of specialty, German was one and either French or Spanish the other. I opted to take Spanish rather than French primarily because there were numerous Spanish-speaking graduate students in our department. No one received the PhD until both exams were passed. Each exam consisted of a general and scientific translation. I had never taken a course in any foreign language. English often seemed foreign to me, and writing was a challenge regardless of subject matter. I enrolled in a non-credit German course and hired a young German tutor who had been in the United States less than a year. I also had a good friend in our department who was from Mexico, and he spent several hours helping me learn Spanish. After much hard work and many long hours, I passed both exams. It was quite an ordeal.

Our second child, James Donald, was born my third year at the Great Graduate School. My major professor always called me Jay, why I don't know, but I liked the name. We decided to call our son Jay and it has stayed that way all these years. I doubt if anybody in town knows his real name.

My PhD program developed rather well, and no storm clouds ever appeared on my horizon. There were times when I wanted to run and hide for a month or so, but that was not possible. Donna remained a constant source of strength and, I might add, income. Her job as a histopathology technician generated enough money for us to stay debt free. My assistantship paid $175 per month, so her work was especially important in keeping us solvent. I remember Donna never complained about her station in life even though we had very little money. New clothes and shoes were put on hold for us since that money needed to go to our children, and that was something we enjoyed doing.

Jeff and I graduated in the summer of 1963 with the PhD in hand. The light at the end of the tunnel was large and bright. Neither of us could believe it was over. We entered the teaching profession at the college level and remained there until retirement. Jeff went back to Kentucky, and I remained in Louisiana. I taught two years at a college in South Louisiana before relocating to my college, Louisiana Tech, in North Louisiana. Jere Mac married Brenda and graduated the following semester. He elected to take an industrial job and remained with industry for ten years. He then accepted a position as a director at LSU, where he enjoyed an outstanding professional reputation. All of us are now retired and still kicking. Peace easy.

7

The Return Home (Phase V)

When I returned to Louisiana Tech, I was hired as a nine-month employee. As a result, my summers were open, which meant I may or may not have a teaching position.

My good friend Stanley, who was a member of our department, suggested I become an agricultural consultant and work with him during the summer months. Stanley had a large business in South Louisiana as a sugarcane consultant. After giving that some thought, I studied for the state entomology exam and passed it on my first attempt. It was a long exam, and difficult, but I was able to pass. As a result, I became a licensed agricultural consultant and worked with Stanley for six years. For the last twelve years of my career, I had my own business and acted as a cotton, soybean, and milo consultant. I was blessed once again because Donna and Jay often worked with me, and it was a family effort.

During my thirty-two years as a college/university professor, many wonderful and good things took place in my life. My department head asked if I would mind working with the wildlife majors. Although I did not major in wildlife, I took the job and established a very active wildlife club. I met many capable students in that capacity, and lasting friendships developed. Two students and I were eventually able to establish a chapter of the National Wildlife Society on our campus and it stayed active for several years.

A master's-level graduate program was now in place in our department, and I was a member of the graduate faculty. Over the years I acted as a major professor for several students, and many of these individuals earned the PhD at other institutions. I am proud of each and every one of them.

As a teacher, thousands of students were members of my classes, and although I am not able to remember all of them, I remember many. My office was always open to all students anytime they wanted to come in for a visit. Faculty members were required to post office hours for student consultations, but I told them to come anytime, I would never be doing anything more important than talking with them. They came, and I was able to meet and make many new and lasting acquaintances. This is when I really got to know them and in a small way pay back that debt I owed. It was awfully rewarding and full of fun. That is the part I miss the most since my retirement.

I wish to relate only one story that took place. I was teaching Introductory Botany, which was a freshman-level course, and one of my students came in for a meeting with me. Botany was not his major but was required in his curriculum, and he was making a very poor grade. As he sat and told me how difficult botany was for him and how it was impossible for him to pass, my thoughts went back to the days when it was difficult for me. Following his confessional, I pulled open my file, withdrew a folder that contained my transcript, and handed it to the student. I then pointed to the semester and the record of my failure in botany. I remember his exact words, which were expressed in shock and dismay: "This is not *your* transcript!" I assured him that it was and that if he would put forth the necessary effort, he could pass my course.

Before my retirement I served as associate dean and director of graduate studies, but that lasted only two years. I requested to be allowed to return to the classroom at the freshmen level, where I felt I had been called to serve. Peace easy.

Epilogue

When the department head at Louisiana Tech called, I was a member of the faculty at the college in South Louisiana, and I listened with mixed emotions. He told me of the untimely death of the man I thought of as the awesome dean. Apparently, he was in a fatal automobile accident while on vacation in a state some distance from Louisiana. As a result of this accident, a vacancy had been created and the department head needed to fill that vacancy with a new teaching position. He then asked if I would be interested in applying for the job. I applied and was subsequently hired as an assistant professor. It was a humbling experience to know I would be occupying a position that had been made available by the awesome dean who had, years before, accepted me into the fold.

Prior to moving back home, Donna and I made a visit to the campus and city looking for a place to build or buy a home. While we were on campus, one of my former art teachers saw me and came over to say hello. I told him I had earned my PhD and would be returning to join the Tech faculty in the Department of Botany and Bacteriology. He was all smiles as he grabbed my arm and escorted me to where the head of the Art Department was standing (the nice lady I talked with that first day of registration) and still smiling, he introduced me as "Doctor White." When I looked down into her eyes, I was also smiling and said, "I guess you are shocked and surprised by this?" She looked at me, not smiling but with a little glint in her eyes, and said, "Not in the least."

After my retirement I authored a book, *Withstanding Storms That Surround*, in which I illustrated seventy-eight historical churches in North and Central Louisiana and included a brief record of their development. I dedicated it as a memorial to my parents. After a public signing at one of our local banks, I was invited by several clubs in the area to be the featured speaker and talk about my book. My high school homeroom teacher, then in her nineties, was in the audience of one of the clubs, and following my presentation, she announced before the entire group, "James, your mother and daddy would be so proud of you!" It caught me by surprise. I guess those old slow-learner feelings surfaced, and all I could say was, "Yes, Ma'am."

During my career at Louisiana Tech University, I was fortunate and blessed in many, many ways. I received several outstanding teaching awards over the years, but I think the best was when I was selected by students as an outstanding teacher on several occasions. I was also pleased to be chosen to appear in an edition of *Outstanding Educators of America.*

One of the nicest and most meaningful awards I ever received took place seven years following my retirement. A former student, practicing medicine in Texas, submitted my name and a short statement to "American Profile," a nationally circulated Sunday supplement. Consequently I, along with six other teachers nationwide, was selected to appear in their cover story in the August 11-17, 2002 edition. A picture of each teacher along with a short story comprised the publication. I thank you, Colton, for remembering me after all these years.

When I was ten or eleven years old, my parents gave me a screw-tail bulldog that I named Duchess. We became the best of friends. My mother had a large old magnolia tree in our front yard that had lower limbs touching the ground. I discovered that if I shook one of those limbs, Duchess would grab hold of the limb's end and not let go. I would swing the limb back and forth and she would hold on until I stopped, walked over, patted her on her head, and told her, "Good job, Duchess." I guess every lower limb on that old magnolia was stripped of terminal leaves, but Mother never complained.

I often told my students about Duchess and the old magnolia tree and then told them that is what they had to do with life—grab hold and don't let go.

So if you are a slow learner, grab hold and don't let go. Someday, somebody will walk up to you, maybe even pat you on your head, and say, "Job well done!"

In closing, I wish to say that it has been difficult for me to share the secrets of my life in this manner. However, if it can be used to assist someone along the way, then for me it has been time well spent. To think I accomplished what is reported in this story on my own merit is absolutely ludicrous. Having professors at the undergraduate and graduate level who took a special interest in me played a major role. Having a wife who believed in me and who always kept the faith was essential. Also, I believe that God provided the strength for me to attain goals I never dreamed possible. I believe He gave me the will and determination to stay in school. It seems obvious to me that God wanted me to be a college professor. I also know that my parents prayed for Donna and me daily and those prayers were answered. Peace easy.

Holden and his mother Laura

Holden and his sister Rachel

Holden in his truck, April 16, 2004

Jeff (left) and James (right) with PhD in hand,

April 1963

About the Author

The author grew up in Ruston, a small town in the hill country of North Louisiana. In his younger years, life was simple, peaceful, and quiet. As he aged, life was no longer simple but complicated by his inability to earn acceptable grades during grammar and high school. Even the first two years at the college level were such a challenge that he almost became a dropout. His inability to learn at a fast rate branded within him the feeling of being a slow learner. This brand would be a part of him his entire life.

But unusual things began to happen during his junior year of college that took over his life and forever changed the downward trend of events. The author is convinced these events were not the result of mere coincidence. When one finds himself or herself at the lowest level of academia, the progressive movement upward seems humanly impossible. Looking back on all the events that resulted in his graduation with the terminal degree, the author can only conclude that it was God's will for that to take place.

With the loss of his sixteen-year-old grandson Holden, who was diagnosed as having dyslexia and attention deficit disorder, the author felt compelled to write his story to give these people hope of greater things to come. Peace easy.